REACH OUT

Tips for Helping
Someone in Crisis

by Jill C. Wheeler

For more information, contact:
ReferencePoint Press, Inc.
PO Box 27779
San Diego, CA 92198
www.ReferencePointPress.com

Content Consultant: Dr. Liliana Burciaga, Assistant Professor of Psychology, Lewis University

LIBRARY OF CONGRESS CATALOGING-IN-PUBLICATION DATA

Names: Wheeler, Jill C., 1964--author.
Title: Reach out: tips for helping someone in crisis / by Jill C. Wheeler.
Description: San Diego, CA: ReferencePoint, [2024] | Includes bibliographical references and index. | Audience: Ages 15-18 | Audience: Grades 10-12
Identifiers: LCCN 2023008715 (print) | LCCN 2023008716 (eBook) | ISBN 9781678205843 (hardcover) | ISBN 9781678205850 (eBook)
Subjects: LCSH: Community psychology--Juvenile literature. | Mental health education--Juvenile literature.
Classification: LCC RA790.55 W44 2024 (print) | LCC RA790.55 (eBook) | DDC 362.2/2--dc23/eng/20230419
LC record available at https://lccn.loc.gov/2023008715
LC eBook record available at https://lccn.loc.gov/2023008716

CONTENTS

Content Warning: This book describes suicide and suicidal thoughts, which may be triggering to some readers.

A Spotlight on Mental Health

In March 2021, Meghan Markle, the Duchess of Sussex and a former actress, and her husband, Prince Harry, the Duke of Sussex, sat down for an exclusive interview. Viewers across the United States tuned in for the much-anticipated event. The two-hour interview covered a variety of topics, including the couple's decision to officially leave their royal duties in 2020.

The interview also included Markle's revelation that there were times in the palace while she was pregnant with her first child that she felt the hopelessness and despair of depression. "I just didn't want to be alive anymore," Markle said. "And that was a very clear and real and frightening constant thought."[1]

At one point, Markle sought mental health help from the palace staff. She said that instead of aiding her, a staff member told her they couldn't help because it wouldn't look good for the monarchy. Markle wanted to tell her husband but felt ashamed of what she was going through. "I know how much loss he suffered," she said, referring to his mother's death when he was a child. "But I knew that if I didn't say it that I would [attempt suicide]."[2]

> "I just didn't want to be alive anymore. And that was a very clear and real and frightening constant thought."
>
> —Meghan Markle, Duchess of Sussex

The UK media often criticized Meghan Markle. This had a negative impact on her mental health.

> "I know how much loss [my husband has] suffered. . . . But I knew that if I didn't say it that I would [attempt suicide]."
> —Meghan Markle, Duchess of Sussex

A Helping Hand

Eventually, Markle opened up to her husband. She found the help she needed thanks to Harry, who referred her to a mental health professional. When calling the woman, Markle explained who she was and told the person she needed help. "She could hear the dire state that I was in," Markle recalled.[3]

With support from Harry and assistance from a professional, Markle was able to get the help she needed. She has been an advocate for mental health awareness and treatment ever since. Markle and Harry have also openly addressed the lack of mental health support from the royal family. This was part of the reason why they decided to leave their royal duties. In a 2022 interview, Harry discussed the negative media coverage that Markle received while in the United Kingdom and how he felt as though his family didn't protect her. "[The royal family] knew how bad it was," Harry said. "They thought, 'Why couldn't she just deal with it?'"[4]

Markle's experience is a high-profile example of how a mental health crisis can happen to anyone—even someone with money, resources, and social status. It is also an example of how a caring individual can make a difference in the life of someone experiencing a mental health crisis. Markle's experience serves as a reminder that mental health can be improved with professional assistance.

Mental health challenges are not unusual. The National Institutes of Health estimates that each year 26 percent of US adults live with a mental illness. However, not everyone gets the help they need. Mental Health America is a nonprofit that advocates for mental health. Research conducted by this organization found that 55 percent of US adults experiencing mental health issues do not receive treatment. When it comes to young people suffering from severe depression, more than 57 percent don't get help. Many factors contribute to this, including access to trained professionals, the ability to pay for the cost of treatment, and lingering stigma about mental illness.

The Power of Caring

A friend, a family member, or even a stranger can provide support to someone suffering from a mental health crisis. Mental health professionals note that expressing care and concern, along with listening without judgment, can be powerful and helpful tools. This is true regardless of the issues behind the crisis. Providing a caring, supportive environment can go a long way in making a difference. In addition, while some people who are having a mental health crisis will reach out for assistance on their own, others may not feel comfortable doing so, or they might not know how to do it. Friends and family members can do their part to reach out and see what kind of help they can give.

It's beneficial for people to educate themselves on mental health issues, including being aware of how common mental illnesses are. Despite the prevalence of mental health disorders, stigmas, which are negative stereotypes, continue to surround these illnesses. These stereotypes stem from false beliefs that are circulated within families and communities, as well as in the media. Stigma can result in discrimination, bullying, and a reluctance to get help, among other things. Education and awareness can help reduce the stigma surrounding mental illness. These things can also help someone feel more comfortable getting help during a mental health crisis.

Adolescents and Mental Illnesses

Approximately 49.5 percent of adolescents in the United States have experienced a mental illness, including anxiety, depression, attention deficit hyperactivity disorder (ADHD), and eating disorders.

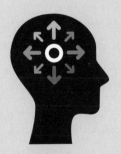

ANXIETY

32 percent of people ages thirteen to eighteen have an anxiety disorder

DEPRESSION

13 percent of people ages twelve to seventeen have depression

ADHD

9 percent of people ages thirteen to eighteen have ADHD

EATING DISORDER

3 percent of people ages thirteen to eighteen have an eating disorder

Source: "Mental Health for Adolescents," OASH, n.d. https://opa.hhs.gov.

CHAPTER ONE

Hidden Struggles

In December 2021, the US surgeon general—the nation's leading public health official—released a report that called attention to mental health issues among adolescents. The report noted that mental health issues among teens had been rising for years. "The challenges today's generation of young people face are unprecedented and uniquely hard to navigate," Surgeon General Dr. Vivek Murthy wrote in the report's introduction. "The effect these challenges have had on their mental health is devastating."[5]

The report pointed to national surveys of youth collected to monitor and evaluate the overall state of adolescent mental health in the country. The surveys showed that the number of high school students who said they often felt sad or hopeless had increased 40 percent between 2009 and 2019. In addition, the report cited statistics from emergency room departments, which noted a 28 percent increase in the number of young people seeking help for anxiety, depression, and problems with behavior between 2011 and 2015.

The surgeon general's report also raised concerns about increases in adolescent suicidal thoughts. National

> "The challenges today's generation of young people face are unprecedented and uniquely hard to navigate. The effect these challenges have had on their mental health is devastating."
>
> —US surgeon general Dr. Vivek Murthy

Dr. Vivek Murthy became the US surgeon general in 2021. One thing he focused on was addressing mental health crises among youth.

surveys from 2009 to 2019 found a 36 percent increase in teens who said they had thought about taking their own lives. Of that group, 44 percent reported they had gone so far as to make a plan on how they would do that. Actual suicide rates also had increased among young people between the ages of ten and twenty-four, rising 57 percent between 2007 and 2018.

Statistics also showed girls were more commonly diagnosed with anxiety, eating disorders, and depression. Boys were more likely than girls to be diagnosed with behavior disorders, including attention deficit hyperactivity disorder (ADHD). They were also more likely to take their own lives.

In addition, LGBTQ+ youth face significant mental health challenges. When compared to their heterosexual peers, lesbian, gay, and bisexual youth are two times more likely to feel persistently hopeless or sad. Transgender youth are two times more likely to have depression and thoughts of suicide. They're also more likely to attempt suicide.

The report also looked at how race and poverty impact mental health. Black children and adolescents had nearly double the suicide rate of their white peers. Young people growing up in low-income households were two to three times more likely than their peers in more affluent households to develop mental health conditions. The surgeon general's report identified financial instability, food shortages, and housing instability as risk factors that contributed to mental health issues in young people. In addition, young people exposed to community violence and

Out of the Darkness

Mental health disorders and the people who suffer from them have long been feared, dismissed, and stigmatized. That has started to change as more people, including celebrities, talk about it openly in the press. Movies and songs also have begun to offer more compassionate portrayals of mental health challenges.

In 2019, singer and actor Selena Gomez collaborated with singer and songwriter Julia Michaels on the song "Anxiety." A few years later, Gomez shared the story of her bipolar disorder diagnosis and treatment in a documentary film, *My Mind & Me*. Other singers have shone the spotlight on mental illness as well. Pop star Taylor Swift released a previously unheard song, "Forever Winter," with her *Red (Taylor's Version)* album in 2021. The song is written from the point of view of someone watching a close friend struggle with mental illness. Singer Demi Lovato went public with her/their own struggles with bulimia, self-harm, and substance abuse with the 2011 song "Skyscraper." Lovato also established a scholarship program to help those who need but cannot afford mental health care. On the fictional side, actors Bradley Cooper and Jennifer Lawrence starred as two people with mental health challenges navigating a new relationship in the 2013 movie *Silver Linings Playbook*.

discrimination had a higher risk of developing mental health problems than peers not dealing with those issues.

Roots of a Crisis

The World Health Organization (WHO) has identified five major influences that impact mental health. These include individual factors such as genetics and age, and also societal factors such as discrimination. Families, communities, and a person's environment play a role too.

Mental health challenges can surface at any stage of life. However, the period from age ten to age nineteen, which is referred to as adolescence, is a particularly sensitive time for mental health issues. Adolescents undergo significant physical changes. They also experience changes in their brains and how they relate to other people and society. The prefrontal cortex, which is the part of the brain that plays the biggest role in making decisions, is not fully developed until a person reaches his or her midtwenties. A developing brain means adolescents are at a higher risk than adults for making decisions that may be unsafe and, in turn, create stress and anxiety.

Mental health issues in teens are relatively common. Statistics indicate that about one in five adolescents has experienced a significant mental health challenge. Oftentimes the stress, insecurity, and hopelessness young people say they experience can be linked back to expectations they may feel from family and peers. Other risk factors for stress and anxiety include the drive many young people have to gain more control over their lives or to be more like their friends. The use of technology, specifically social media, can also impact a person's mental health.

More Than Mood Swings

Experts have identified three categories of mental health challenges that teens frequently experience: anxiety, social phobia, and depression. In the first category, anxiety, people may become anxious when experiencing major life events or even everyday situations. For instance, upcoming tests, first dates, jobs, and college decisions may trigger anxiety.

Anxiety is a common part of life, and most people will experience it from time to time. Mental health professionals consider anxiety to be an issue when it begins to interfere with daily activities. Feelings of anxiety that last a long time, that people have a hard time controlling, or that seem disproportionally severe to the situation at hand can be signs of an anxiety disorder. Children and teens may experience symptoms of anxiety differently than adults. For instance, they may have stomachaches and headaches, they may be easily irritated, and they may have a hard time concentrating. Other symptoms of anxiety include feeling nervous or having a hard time not worrying.

The second category is social anxiety disorder, or social phobia. People with this disorder are anxious, embarrassed,

Fighting Stigma

People who have mental illnesses are sometimes blamed for their disorders. They're told to snap out of it or that they're not really trying to feel better. People sometimes call them names or don't want to be around them. These are all examples of how stigma causes one group of people to treat another badly.

Stigma makes people feel embarrassed about their mental illness. It may stop people from reaching out for help. Luna Greenstein works at the National Alliance on Mental Illness (NAMI). She notes, "For a group of people who already carry such a heavy burden, stigma is an unacceptable addition to their pain. . . . All of us in the mental health community need to raise our voices against stigma. Every day, in every possible way, we need to stand up to stigma."

One way to fight stigma is to be open about what it's like living with a mental health condition. This helps educate people. It also shows people who have a disorder that they're not alone. Other ways to fight stigma include showing compassion and calling out people or media when they make stigmatizing comments.

Luna Greenstein, "9 Ways to Fight Mental Health Stigma," NAMI, October 11, 2017. www.nami.org.

People with depression may find it difficult to get out of bed. This could hurt their relationships and performance at school and work.

and self-conscious when it comes to everyday interactions. They fear people are judging and forming negative opinions about them. It's normal for people to experience a few jitters in social situations. The feelings become a mental health concern when they disrupt people's lives and relationships. For instance, people with this disorder may avoid specific events where they might feel embarrassed, judged, or evaluated.

The final category is depression. Occasionally feeling sad is normal, but depression interferes with a person's day-to-day life. People with this mood disorder may feel sad, empty, and hopeless. They may have little interest in the things they once enjoyed. They might sleep or eat too much or too little. People with depression might also have suicidal thoughts.

Depression often looks different in younger people than it does in adults. Children may act irritable, or they may be clingy with those around them. Kids and teens with depression might not want to go to school, and their grades may suffer. Teens might also become angry. They may act out in unsafe ways through self-harm, such as cutting themselves, or by using drugs or alcohol. Megan Shinnick suffered from depression as a teen. "Even though I was incredibly academically motivated in the past, I couldn't seem to do homework. And I removed myself from friends, and I didn't answer my phone for a week. And I refused to go to school. And getting out of bed in the morning seemed impossible," she explained.[6]

Adding Fuel to the Fire

Research has found that loneliness is an important factor in depression and thoughts of suicide. And while people seem more connected than ever thanks to the internet, teens may feel lonely even if they talk to people online. "They're hanging out with friends, but no friends are there," explains psychologist Bonnie Nagel. "It's not the same social connectedness we need and not the kind that prevents one from feeling lonely."[7] Research shows that real-life relationships play an important role in creating the connected feeling people need for good mental health.

Social media may create stressful situations too. Getting cyberbullied on social media can have a negative impact on a person's mental health. Social media may also amplify existing concerns teens might have about their body image or social status. One study found that typical teen mental health challenges appeared to be worse for those who spent more time on social media. Researchers note that social media and other online activities probably have this effect because they are more likely to amplify existing feelings of distress. Dr. Vivek Murthy explains, "Young people

> "They're hanging out with friends, but no friends are there. It's not the same social connectedness we need and not the kind that prevents one from feeling lonely."
>
> —Bonnie Nagel, psychologist

are bombarded with messages through the media and popular culture that erode their sense of self-worth—telling them they are not good-looking enough, popular enough, smart enough or rich enough."[8]

People's mental health has a major influence on how they feel about themselves and others. Mental health is a factor in how well people solve problems and handle stress. Good mental health makes it easier for people to address challenges without emotional outbursts, fighting, or undesirable coping mechanisms, such as using drugs or alcohol. The quality of relationships and academic and professional success also hinges on the state of an individual's mental health.

A Hopeful Future

Acting early can reduce the intensity of a mental health crisis and help prevent the situation from worsening. "Timely interventions are imperative. If not diagnosed early, the clinical onset of mental illness during adolescence can lead to difficult-to-treat chronic mental illness throughout adulthood," says Dr. Holly Farley.[9]

A pandemic started in 2020 after people around the world began getting sick with a disease called COVID-19. The pandemic intensified and amplified factors that may trigger a mental health crisis, including financial instability, food shortages, and housing instability. Moving forward, mental health advocates are urging communities and governments to learn from this experience. Minimizing known risk factors and developing more available and accessible resources for help remain the best measures to prevent mental health issues among young people.

> "Timely interventions are imperative. If not diagnosed early, the clinical onset of mental illness during adolescence can lead to difficult-to-treat chronic mental illness throughout adulthood."
> —Dr. Holly Farley

CHAPTER TWO

Preparing to Reach Out

In order to reach out and help someone in a mental health crisis, the first step is to become aware that the person is struggling. Social awareness involves understanding and empathizing with other people's emotions. It's an essential skill needed to recognize when someone is in need. Social

Special Skills Not Required

While friends and family are often the first people to reach out to someone in crisis, strangers can also make a difference. Researchers in the United Kingdom interviewed two groups of people. One group of people had been stopped from taking their own lives in a public place by the intervention of a stranger. The other group were ordinary people who had intervened to successfully prevent a suicide in a public place.

Analysis of the interviews concluded that complete strangers could indeed help prevent people from taking their own lives. The strangers who intervened shared several common traits, including a high level of social awareness and a willingness to act on their feelings. No special skills were required. Rather, the strangers who were successful were able to connect with the person in crisis, get him or her to move to a safer location, and then call for professional assistance. Interviewees who had been stopped from killing themselves credited the strangers with helping them feel safe and connected to others. The survivors also said the strangers had made them feel that their lives mattered.

People can help their friends navigate through difficult times. They can pay attention to their friends' behaviors and reach out if they're worried.

awareness is one of four elements of emotional intelligence, along with self-awareness, self-management, and relationship management. Emotionally intelligent people are aware of their own feelings and the feelings of others.

Everyone can improve their social awareness skills by learning how to be observant and a good listener. Practicing these two things may be as simple as someone slowing down and taking the time to observe what is happening around him instead of focusing only on what he is doing. Research has found that people can easily overlook things that are right in front of them if they aren't paying attention. To help someone who is having a mental health crisis, caring friends and family first need to pay close attention to that person in order to see signs that he or she is struggling. They may want to observe whether the person is sleeping or eating more or less than usual. People can also pay attention to see if the person has pulled back from activities he or she used to enjoy. Slipping grades and avoidance of certain situations or people are other signs someone is struggling with mental health. People can also observe whether the person has started to use drugs or alcohol more than usual or if the person exhibits aggressive behaviors, such as anger or yelling. All of these signs suggest that someone might need help.

Social awareness also can mean learning to read the nonverbal signs that people give off through body language, including expressions on their faces. Research has indicated that up to 55 percent of communication is through body language. For instance, when talking to an individual who may be struggling with her mental health, friends can pay attention to whether she looks them in the eye when talking. Looking away could mean she is feeling nervous or anxious. In addition, a forced smile that does not reach the eyes could mean someone is pretending to be happy when she really isn't.

Differences in a Crisis

Individuals with strong social awareness skills are better able to put themselves in another's shoes to see how the world might look from the other person's perspective. This is a valuable skill when it comes to getting more insight into what's happening with someone who may be going through a mental health crisis. The more people can understand what a person is going through, the better they can help identify resources that might help the person. "It's compassion, listening, showing genuine interest in what people are going through and experiencing," explains psychiatrist Elia Abi-Jaoude. "It makes a world of a difference."[10]

A mental health crisis may look different from person to person. It can depend on a person's age, gender, or cultural or socioeconomic background. Additionally, some individuals may grow up in families or cultures where mental health

> "It's compassion, listening, showing genuine interest in what people are going through and experiencing. It makes a world of a difference."
> —Dr. Elia Abi-Jaoude, psychiatrist

issues are discussed openly. Others may grow up in families or cultures that shy away from such discussions. How a person facing a mental health crisis reacts to his or her situation can therefore be different based on these factors.

There are gender differences when it comes to mental health challenges. Statistics indicate that girls are more likely to be diagnosed with internalizing disorders, such as anxiety and depression. Boys are more likely to be diagnosed with externalizing disorders. These disorders have their roots in impulsive behaviors such as aggression, rule breaking, and acting out.

Some researchers attribute these gender differences to the way girls and boys are typically socialized. Girls may grow up believing they have less power and less worth outside traditional feminine roles of nurturing and caretaking. This may cause them to internalize their own mental health challenges. Internalizing involves turning problematic feelings inward, literally against one's own self.

Boys are more likely to grow up believing that they have more power and more worth. They may feel more comfortable in the external world but uncomfortable with feelings, especially those that may be regarded as not masculine. This leads to a tendency to externalize mental health challenges. That may involve directing problematic feelings outward, often in the form of substance abuse or antisocial behaviors that can harm others.

LGBTQ+ individuals also face mental health challenges. Stigma around LGBTQ+ people may lead members of this community to experience and then internalize shame about who they are. This can lead to heightened levels of anxiety and depression. In addition to facing cultural stigmas, LGBTQ+ individuals are at a higher risk of being victims of discrimination, harassment, and assault. These experiences may lead to anxiety and depression. They may also cause post-traumatic stress disorder and other trauma-related long-term mental health challenges.

Certain environmental risk factors have been shown to increase suicidal thoughts and behaviors. While these factors are no guarantee that someone exposed to them will become suicidal, they can be important clues that someone may be under stress. Research has found that people who have family members or peers who have either attempted or died by suicide are at greater risk of developing those behaviors themselves. Problems with drug and alcohol abuse have also been identified as a risk factor, along with access to firearms. Exposure to violence in the home or at school is another risk factor.

Research has identified multiple groups that have a greater risk of going through mental health challenges. These groups include those with a family history of mental illness, people who

LGBTQ+ stands for lesbian, gay, bisexual, transgender, and queer/questioning. These individuals are much more likely to experience bullying and violence than people who aren't LGBTQ+.

live in lower-income households, people of color, LGBTQ+ people, and individuals who have a disability. For some of these groups, such as minority populations or LGBTQ+ individuals, the increased risk is due to the higher levels of discrimination and victimization they face compared to other groups. This increases their risk of developing mental illnesses and showing suicidal behaviors.

Other groups are at increased risk due to reduced access to mental health care or other barriers to care, such as cultural stigmas, that discourage people from getting help. One example of a barrier is the distrust of medical providers experienced by some people within the Black community due to a history of racial bias and discrimination.

An added barrier for many Black people is a stigma around getting mental health care that has been linked to years of racism

The Tuskegee Study

Black people have been exploited by medical professionals in the past. For instance, between 1932 and 1972, hundreds of Black men who had syphilis joined a scientific study called the Tuskegee Study. Researchers enticed Black men to participate by promising things that weren't widely available to them, such as free medical exams and free care for minor illnesses. The men never knew the true nature of the study or were informed of the consequences for either getting or not getting treatment. Untreated syphilis can damage people's organs and kill them. For those who did get treatment, they were often given toxic substances such as mercury and arsenic. When penicillin became available to treat syphilis in 1947, the men did not receive it. Planned Parenthood explains why: "Because of their race, the men in the study were viewed and treated as less-than human. They were used as research subjects, much like rats, whose sole purpose was to reveal the long-term effects of this potentially deadly disease." The Tuskegee Study is one reason why some Black people don't trust medical professionals.

"What Is the Tuskegee Study?" Planned Parenthood, *November 12, 2021. www.plannedparenthood.org.*

and oppression. Ruth White is an associate professor at the University of Southern California. She says, "Much of the pushback against seeking treatment stems from the ideas along the lines of: We have survived so much adversity and now someone is going to say that there's something wrong with us."[11]

Members of the Latino community may also face stigma related to getting mental health care, though the reasons may be slightly different. Some people in the Latino community believe that mental health issues should remain private and within a family to prevent embarrassment and shame for the family. In addition, language barriers, lack of health insurance, concerns about legal status, and a lack of health care providers who understand Latino culture can also create obstacles for some Latino individuals.

Many barriers can be overcome through better education, resources, and cross-cultural understanding. Being a member of a high-risk group does not mean that a person will develop a mental illness. But friends and family can keep these risk factors and obstacles in the backs of their minds. That way, they may be able to better identify if someone they care about is struggling.

> "Much of the pushback against seeking treatment stems from the ideas along the lines of: We have survived so much adversity and now someone is going to say that there's something wrong with us."
>
> —Ruth White, associate professor at the University of Southern California

Giving Support

People should always reach out to professionals when it comes to getting help for mental health challenges. People who are trained in mental health and crisis management can aid a struggling person and provide him or her with resources to get a crisis under control. For instance, psychologists, counselors, therapists, and more are trained to recognize and handle behavioral and emotional issues. They use tested scientific techniques to teach people how to handle their emotions, such as managing stress, and how to make healthy goals and work toward them. This makes mental health professionals important resources for someone going through a mental health crisis.

Friends and family are well-positioned to help a person experiencing a crisis take those critical first steps to getting the professional assistance he or she needs. That's because they may be among those most likely to see the signs of a potential or current mental health challenge. Also, having a caring and trusting relationship makes it more likely that the person experiencing the crisis can be encouraged to take action. Luna Greenstein works at the National Alliance on Mental Illness (NAMI). She notes:

> When de-escalating someone from crisis, communication is key. It is essential they feel heard and understood, so make sure to give them your undivided attention. This is more than just listening, but also using body language, like eye contact, to show you're listening. You can also use active listening techniques—such as reflecting feelings and summarizing thoughts—to help them feel validated.[12]

Mental health professionals note that people should take stock of their own situation before offering to help someone in a crisis. Being supportive requires energy, commitment, and, ideally, an understanding of what that support involves. It is important to be realistic about how much time, energy, and assistance people are able to provide.

Before reaching out to someone, people can ask themselves if they are in a position to help the individual for potentially a long time. Many mental health challenges require extended treatment. While mental health professionals are used to this, it may be a new situation for friends and family members to see the person they care about struggling for a long time, even when he or she is getting professional help. Family and friends can also reach out to others who care about the person. Together, they can share the mental, emotional, and sometimes logistical work that comes with being supportive.

Mental health professionals also suggest that caring friends and family members create a plan of action before trying to help. This plan could include pulling together contact information for professional resources including hotlines, emergency rooms, walk-in crisis centers, and health care professionals. Family and friends can include their own contact information, plus that of

Being Heard

Australian mental health advocacy organization batyr, which is purposefully spelled lowercase, teaches young people how to talk about and share their experiences with mental health. The batyr Being Herd program includes a workshop, an app, and online and in-person communities. Being Herd builds on research showing that people who talk openly about their mental health issues can often encourage others to address their own challenges by showing them that getting mental health help leads to a better life. Sharing stories may also help the speakers realize things about their own experiences that they might have missed before.

Researchers were curious what impact the Being Herd program had on peers who interacted with people telling their stories. Researchers found that discussing mental health issues led to positive results in both prevention and treatment of mental health issues among listeners. "Creating an environment where young people feel comfortable talking about mental health is a step forward towards the normalization of these conversations," the researchers reported.

Genesis Lindstrom, Ernesta Sofija, and Tom Riley, "'Getting Better at Getting Better:' How Sharing Mental Health Stories Can Shape Young People's Wellbeing," Community Mental Health Journal, *February 12, 2021. https://link.springer.com.*

others who have agreed to help. The more people who are in on the plan, the greater the chance that someone will be available to talk or text the person who needs support when necessary.

It's also important that people know and set their own boundaries when helping someone through a crisis. This helps people protect their own mental health. For instance, helpers can determine whether they're OK with someone calling them in the middle of the night for support, or while they're at school or work. Helpers should keep in mind what they are and aren't willing to do and make that clear to the person they want to help. It's okay to tell the person when it's appropriate to contact them. Helpers can also encourage the person to think about who he might call if he needs to talk when they're unavailable.

In addition to setting boundaries, supportive friends and family should make a plan to take care of themselves. They may need their own support system as they help someone else to avoid feeling burned out. They can think in advance about what things make them feel better, whether it is a hot bath, watching a movie, or spending time with special people. Then they should watch their energy levels and step back if they feel themselves becoming overwhelmed.

If family members or friends do need to take a break from supporting someone in a crisis, they can do that without risking the trust they have carefully built. The key is clear and thoughtful communication. If helpers realize they're overwhelmed, it's best to be honest about it. They should communicate in a way that neither blames nor shames the person in crisis. They can work with the person to identify other people in her support system to whom she can turn. In addition, overwhelmed helpers can set a date for when they will check up on the person. Then they need to keep that promise. No one likes to feel abandoned, especially if they are experiencing a crisis.

The severity of a mental health crisis plays a role in how people should respond. A key factor in how situations are handled is whether people are currently a danger to themselves. If there is a threat or an attempt of suicide or other self-harming behaviors,

One form of treatment may include group therapy. People open up about their own struggles and hear what others are going through.

the situation should be treated as a medical emergency. It's also a medical emergency when individuals are posing a threat to others.

Treatment options vary based on the situation and severity of the mental health crisis. Treatment can take place at the individual's home, or at inpatient or outpatient mental health facilities. Outpatient facilities are where patients go during the day to get help from trained medical professionals. Inpatient facilities require patients to live there during treatment. Treatment may also begin in an emergency room.

Not everyone will be open to acknowledging a need for professional help or accepting that help. In those situations, it can be useful to talk to the person in crisis about the benefits of getting help. For example, some mental health professionals working with men resistant to mental health help have been encouraged to focus on treatment as an opportunity for the men to get strong or to become well. It can also be useful to focus on concrete problems someone may be having and offer professional help as a way to better address those problems, such as trouble sleeping or trouble focusing on homework.

CHAPTER THREE

Starting a Conversation

It's important to understand that mental illness can be treated. People may experience a range of mental health issues throughout their lives. Some mental health challenges are short-term and may create mostly minor disruptions within a person's day-to-day activities. Other challenges may create significant disruptions to someone's daily life for an extended period of time. These are important things to keep in mind when starting a conversation aimed at helping someone get through a mental health crisis.

Before starting a conversation, people need to realize that it's not their job to solve a crisis. As a person reaching out, the goal is to help connect the person experiencing a crisis to resources that can identify the right path of action for his or her unique situation. People reaching out can be more successful doing that if they show they care about the person and actively listen to him or her.

While every crisis situation is different, mental health experts agree on several basic guidelines when it comes to conversations with someone who may be in crisis. For instance, it is OK and necessary to ask difficult questions. If people have reason to be concerned that the person in crisis might engage in self-harm, it is OK to ask whether the person has thought about taking his or her life. People should be assured that talking with someone about suicidal thoughts does not make someone more likely to harm themselves. "Most people are afraid to ask about suicide, because

People struggling with their mental health can seek out professional assistance. Professionals such as therapists can help people develop skills to live happy, healthy lives.

they don't want to put the thought in their head. But there's no research to support that," said psychologist Doreen Marshall.[13]

In addition, place and time play a role. If possible, helpers should seek to have a conversation in a place where the person in crisis feels as safe and comfortable as possible. Sometimes that means going to an area that is not associated with a home, school, or other place where stressful issues can arise. Other times, a caring friend or family member might need to act in the moment, regardless of the place, if the person in crisis is considering self-harm.

"Most people are afraid to ask about suicide, because they don't want to put the thought in their head. But there's no research to support that."

—Doreen Marshall, psychologist

Opening a Door

If a helper regularly participates in the same activities as the person who may be in crisis, it can be beneficial to start the conversation in conjunction with those joint activities. Casual questions about how someone is doing can feel less overwhelming when asked in a familiar environment. If the two people do not typically do joint activities, it can still be a good idea for a friend to invite another to join him or her in a hobby or special event. The invitation can show that the person cares while creating an opportunity for focused time together.

Experts also suggest helpers keep in mind that talking about personal issues is easier for some people than others. Some individuals may need more time to open up about what is on their minds. Others may be eager to share their situations with someone they trust. Friends and family members should be

Exercise improves both mental and physical health. Spending time with friends can also have a positive effect on a person's mental health.

prepared to watch for body language and other clues during the conversation. If someone looks agitated or puzzled, it can be a sign to slow down or to be more direct in asking questions.

Regardless of when and where the conversation begins, helpers should be prepared to be patient but persistent. They should make it a point to remind the person in crisis that they care about him or her. "Be gentle, be curious, and, over time, be persistent but not insistent," says teen mental health expert Stephen Hinshaw.[14]

Helpers should give the person in crisis time to think and process his or her thoughts and emotions. They should remember how difficult it can be to talk about strong feelings. Some people may take a long time to respond to specific questions. Helpers should be patient and not afraid to gently repeat a question if they have not heard a response.

Active Listening

Mental health advocates recommend a style of conversation called active listening. This type of listening means people should make the conversation the center of their attention. They should put their phones down and turn off other distractions, such as televisions, if possible. They should face the person they're talking with and maintain eye contact during the conversation. All of these practices signal that the listener is engaged and cares about what the person who is struggling has to say.

Another important aspect of active listening involves asking questions. People should avoid asking simple "yes" or "no" questions. Instead of asking, "Do you feel OK?" a person might ask, "What can you tell me about how you're feeling?" Open-ended questions typically lead to more follow-up discussions and richer conversations. For example, if someone talks about a specific thing that happened to him or her that day, a follow-up question could be, "What does that mean to you?"

Active listening also involves briefly summarizing what the person is hearing. From time to time, the listener should repeat key items he or she has heard during the conversation. This helps show that he or she understands what the other person is talking about. It also communicates that the person is actively engaged and interested in the other person's situation. Writer Arlin Cuncic explains why active listening is important: "It keeps you engaged with your conversation partner in a positive way. It also makes the other person feel heard and valued. This skill is the foundation of a successful conversation in any setting—whether at work, at home, or in social situations."[15]

Listening vs. Problem Solving

When approaching someone who seems to be struggling, helpers should keep in mind that the person might be in the midst of an intense mental health crisis, such as thinking about taking his or her life. It may also be possible that the person is experiencing a panic attack or has had an unusually difficult day. This may have intensified an existing anxiety but not in a life-threatening way.

How It Feels: Panic Attack

A panic attack is a feeling of intense fear that comes on very suddenly and is usually accompanied by physical symptoms. Panic attacks can happen at any time and often occur for unknown reasons. Symptoms can include a racing heart, dizziness, chest pain, and sweating. Most panic attacks last between five and twenty minutes. The intensity of the feeling can leave a person shaken and exhausted.

First-person reports of panic attacks offer a glimpse into what this mental health condition feels like. A man named Carl noted that during his panic attacks he "sincerely feared [he was] at risk of keeling over and dying in the gutter." A man named Jonathan has had panic attacks for years and said while having them, "My heart starts pounding so hard that it feels like I'm going to have a heart attack, yet there is no physical pain." Lindsey described the frightening feeling of her panic attacks: "I feel like I can't breathe— almost as if I'm being held underwater with no way of coming up for air."

Tessa Miller, "9 People Describe What It Feels Like to Have a Panic Attack," Self, *October 28, 2017. www.self.com.*

In any case, active listening can help someone feel that he or she is being heard and understood.

People may be tempted to jump into conversations and offer quick solutions. But experts caution that listening is more important than problem-solving. Asking the right questions can help guide the person in crisis to insights that will allow him or her to see potential next steps toward getting help. For example, a helper might suggest that it can be beneficial when in a crisis to talk to someone who has been through a similar experience. Helpers can then directly ask if the person in crisis knows someone who has been through something similar whom he or she can talk with.

Helpers should also be prepared to be flexible. Sometimes people in crisis would prefer to talk with their parents or other trusted adults instead of the original person reaching out. In that case, the helper can ask what he or she can do to assist the person in connecting with others. Asking whom the person in crisis has gone to before with different problems or challenges can also help him or her identify alternate sources of assistance.

If a helper has noticed behaviors of concern, it is acceptable to express those concerns before asking what is happening emotionally. Saying "I've been worried about you" or "I'm concerned about your safety" communicates that a person cares. Helpers can follow up those questions with open-ended ones such as, "Can we talk about what you are experiencing?"

Sometimes people don't always know the perfect things to say. But experts note that simply reaching out is beneficial. "Even if you can't find the exact words [to say], the aspect that somebody cares makes a big difference," said psychologist DeQuincy Lezine.[16]

> "Even if you can't find the exact words [to say], the aspect that somebody cares makes a big difference."
>
> —DeQuincy Lezine, psychologist

At first, people may not fully understand why their friend acts a certain way. Listening without judgment can give them insight into how their friend is feeling.

Avoiding Judgment

Once the conversation gets started, mental health experts encourage helpers to remain open and calm. Being nonjudgmental is also critical. Feeling judged can have a negative impact when the person having a crisis is trying to open up. Even if a helper disagrees with what the person has done or said, it's important to remain focused on the person and on getting her the help she needs. People who feel judged and shamed are less likely to be open about what they are going through.

It can be helpful to focus on empathy. For example, perhaps a helper suspects someone has been skipping classes. It would be easy to tell the person that cutting class is a bad idea and that he or she should feel guilty for doing that. Instead, helpers can work on being curious and open-minded. They should not assume that they know what someone else is thinking. Helpers should try to see the situation from that person's perspective. A person in crisis may have reasons for skipping class that a helper does not know about.

Similarly, helpers should avoid telling someone that his feelings and concerns are no big deal. Even if helpers think someone is overreacting, they need to put that opinion aside and listen patiently. They can remind the person in crisis that what he is experiencing is not his fault. Helpers can acknowledge that even if they do not understand what the person is going through, they are still there to help. In fact, it's unlikely a helper will know exactly what someone else is experiencing. But experts say that is not necessary in order to help. "Try not to figure out what the 'right' thing to say is," says therapist Larry Shushansky. "Just be caring and concerned and let that show through in your conversation."[17] Helpers can offer assistance instead of advice.

> "Try not to figure out what the 'right' thing to say is. Just be caring and concerned and let that show through in your conversation."
>
> —Larry Shushansky, therapist

Sometimes a thoughtful, caring conversation is enough to prevent an emergency situation. It can also help direct people in crisis to the professional resources that can help them. Other times, it might be necessary for a person to get immediate professional assistance. For instance, helpers may need to call 911 or a suicide prevention hotline while they are with the person in crisis. They can also call 988, which is the National Suicide Prevention Lifeline. It is also OK for helpers to speak directly with a crisis hotline and get professional advice for next steps in their particular situation.

Mental health experts suggest that people considering suicide should not be left alone. If helpers are unable to stay with the person in crisis, they can reach out to another responsible and caring figure in the person's life for assistance. They can also work with a crisis hotline to identify alternative actions.

Pitching In

Caring conversations are critical to effectively reach out to someone in crisis. There are other ways to help as well. Sometimes it can be as simple as offering assistance with errands or chores. For example, a helper might offer to watch a friend's younger sibling so the friend is free to meet with a counselor. Helpers can also offer someone a ride to go talk to a professional or take the person to a crisis center. The person may want the helper to hang out in a waiting room with her while she waits to talk with someone. All of those scenarios are ways to directly support someone in crisis.

Support doesn't need to be limited to helping a person in crisis access mental health assistance. Inviting someone to coffee, providing a meal when she is feeling overwhelmed, or even bringing flowers all show that a person cares. These simple

How It Feels: Depression

Depression is a mood disorder commonly associated with ongoing, intense sadness. It's a complex mental health challenge that can affect each person differently. Depression might cause one person to stay in his bed. It might cause another to be out of her home frequently in order to avoid being alone.

Depression can be described in a number of ways. Dr. Anjani Amladi is a psychiatrist. Amladi notes, "Depression robs people of things they once loved, and for many people, they feel like nothing will bring them joy again." Amladi also notes that depression "can lead to a feeling of exhaustion and low energy which can prevent people from even being able to get out of bed, or perform daily activities like showering, eating and brushing their teeth."

Sara Lindberg, "What Does Depression Feel Like?" Very Well Mind, November 29, 2022. www.verywellmind.com.

gestures are important ways to support people not only during a crisis but also as they work their way through any necessary treatment or therapy. Committing to regular check-ins, even if only through text messaging, is another way to show support.

Driving a friend to visit a mental health professional is one way helpers can show they care.

CHAPTER FOUR

Caring Connections

Help for people experiencing a mental health crisis is available in multiple forms depending on the urgency of the situation. These include phone and text lines. Emergency rooms, 911, care centers, and peer-run crisis lines are other important resources.

If someone is considering taking his or her own life, immediate help is available by dialing or texting 988 to reach the National Suicide Prevention Lifeline. This free, confidential support line is available twenty-four hours a day, seven days a week. The line accepts calls from people of all ages.

Once connected, callers will hear a brief recording to guide them to the right area of assistance. The Lifeline is a collection of more than 160 crisis centers located around the United States, so the system routes callers to the center nearest them. Once there, callers are connected to staff members who may be either mental health professionals or trained volunteers.

While each conversation on the Lifeline is unique, Lifeline professionals focus on creating a safe and comfortable environment. Callers direct the conversation based on what they feel like sharing. Staff members may ask questions to help pinpoint the most helpful resources. A key role of the Lifeline staffers is helping people access some of their own resources. "When a person is in a crisis state, they are so overwhelmed by the psychic pain they're experiencing—it's really hard for them to see all options and actually engage

Sometimes people need encouragement to reach out for help. Caring friends can familiarize themselves with the different mental health resources available.

some of their natural coping mechanisms," says Lifeline executive director Dr. John Draper.[18]

> "When a person is in a crisis state, they are so overwhelmed by the psychic pain they're experiencing—it's really hard for them to see all options and actually engage some of their natural coping mechanisms."
>
> —Dr. John Draper, Lifeline executive director

Lifeline staffers also take calls from people who are looking to help someone else. For instance, if an individual is concerned about someone who is talking about suicide, he or she can call the Lifeline. The caller can then talk with someone who has been trained on what to do in that situation.

Crisis Text Line

For those who prefer outreach via text message or messaging app, the Crisis Text Line can be accessed by texting HOME to 741741 on a mobile phone, or to 443-SUPPORT via WhatsApp. After texting or messaging for the first time, the Crisis Text Line will send an automated response asking about the nature of the crisis. That information helps the line connect the texter to the appropriate crisis counselor, who responds via text message.

The Crisis Text Line provides mental health support twenty-four hours a day, seven days a week. While the counseling is offered free of charge, text messaging rates do apply. Several large mobile carriers, however, offer free texting to the 741741 number.

Emergency Rooms and 911

Calling 911 or taking someone to an emergency room may be options if the person is talking about harming themselves or others. This is also an option if the individual has already engaged in self-harming behaviors, such as cutting. Overdosing or alcohol poisoning are other reasons to get someone medical help right away.

Someone having suicidal thoughts should go to the hospital. Health care workers can assess the person and connect him with a mental health professional.

It is acceptable to take people to an emergency room without their consent if they are in urgent need of medical assistance, such as in an overdose situation. If people are not in a life-threatening situation, it is best to get their agreement before reaching out to these services. This is because treatments tend to be more effective when the person in crisis has agreed to get help. When calling 911, a person can explain that he or she is seeking help from someone with experience in crisis intervention. The helper can offer to stay with the person in crisis while waiting for assistance.

Health Care Professionals

Not everyone has a relationship with a doctor, nurse practitioner, or other licensed health care professional. However, for those who do, these individuals can be excellent sources for help and referrals in a time of crisis. Helpers can ask the person in crisis if there is a doctor, nurse, or counselor whom he sees regularly and might be able to assist him. Family members of the person in crisis may also have connections that can be useful.

Some mental health professionals advocate for increased collaboration between primary care providers (PCPs) and mental health professionals due to the PCP's role on the front lines of helping patients. "The fact is that most mental health problems are presenting in primary care," says Carol Alter, a behavioral health medical director in Dallas, Texas. "There are things that can be done to help the primary care doctors diagnose and do that better. It's not only doable, it's actually where primary care is going."[19]

> "The fact is that most mental health problems are presenting in primary care. . . . There are things that can be done to help the primary care doctors diagnose and do that better. It's not only doable, it's actually where primary care is going."
>
> —Carol Alter, a behavioral health medical director

Substance Abuse and Mental Health Care Centers

Some communities have professionals who specialize in helping people with mental illnesses, substance abuse, and related challenges. These services can be provided on an outpatient basis, such as telehealth visits or visiting the office of a therapist, or on an inpatient basis, such as participating in a residential treatment program at a special facility outside one's home. The US government's Substance Abuse and Mental Health Services Administration (SAMHSA) has a Behavioral Health Treatment Services Locator. This online tool allows people to find health care professionals near them. Both helpers and people in crisis can look for nearby providers at https://findtreatment.samhsa.gov. Searches are confidential, meaning it is not necessary for people to identify themselves.

SAMHSA also has a National Helpline and a text messaging service. These services are for people who may not have internet access or who wish to access resources through their phone. The National Helpline operates twenty-four hours a day, seven days a

Telehealth Takes Off

Telehealth uses technology such as video conferencing services to connect people with health care professionals, including behavioral health providers. Telehealth service options made major gains during the COVID-19 pandemic. Use of telehealth visits for mental health services in the United States grew more than 550 percent in the early months of the pandemic compared to prepandemic levels.

Telehealth is an increasingly important component of mental health services for rural residents who may not have access to psychiatrists, psychologists, and therapists locally. For people who want to help someone seek out mental health services, it is worth asking if telehealth is an option for the person. He or she will need access to a computer or tablet with broadband internet, or a mobile phone, in order to take advantage of telehealth services.

week, at 1-800-662-HELP (4357). People can also send a text with their zip code to the service at 435748 (HELP4U).

The SAMHSA services are referral services, not counselors. SAMHSA staffers are trained to help locate professional counselors in local communities. They are a good option when the crisis is not life-threatening.

Teachers and Community Leaders

Mental health professionals are critical resources for people experiencing a crisis. Yet the US Health Resources and Services Administration reports that nearly 40 percent of the US population lives in an area where there is a shortage of mental health providers. When it's not possible to reach such professionals, it might be feasible to seek help from others who may have received basic training in mental health issues. These can include professionals in an education setting, such as school counselors, school psychologists, and school social workers.

Teachers, parents, and coaches are often good people to connect with when trying to find help too. In addition, media specialists such as librarians may be another option. These people might be able to help identify sources of assistance, such as finding a primary care physician. Contacting a primary care physician is a good place to start when looking for a referral to a mental health provider.

Peer-Run Crisis Lines

Peer-run crisis lines are an additional resource available for young people in crisis. Similar to other crisis lines, these resources use trained volunteers to answer phone calls, text or chat messages, or emails from teens looking for someone to talk to. The key difference is that the volunteers themselves are teens and other young people, although mental health professionals supervise them.

Hours for these help lines vary. They are not always open twenty-four hours per day, seven days a week. One example of a peer-run crisis line is Youth Line. It can be reached by texting teen2teen to 839863 or calling 1-877-968-8491.

Teen Link (1-866-833-6546) is another resource. It accepts calls, chats, and texts. Another resource, Teen Line, can be reached at 1-800-852-8336 or by texting TEEN to 839863.

Specialized Hotlines for At-Risk People

In addition to basic crisis lines, there are specialized hotlines for several groups of people who experience statistically higher rates of mental health crises. Groups experiencing these higher rates include veterans, LGBTQ+ individuals, Indigenous peoples, and victims of rape and incest. Like other crisis lines, specialized hotlines are confidential and free of charge.

LGBTQ+ individuals can access the Trans Lifeline (1-877-565-8860) and the Trevor Lifeline (1-866-488-7386). Veterans and active-duty military personnel can contact the Veteran's Crisis Line via 988, option 1, or text the Crisis Chat at 838255. The National Sexual Assault Hotline can be accessed at 1-800-656-HOPE (4673).

Robot Therapists

Advances in artificial intelligence are allowing computers to potentially help people with their mental health concerns. Mobile apps such as Woebot, which was designed by psychologists at Stanford University, claim to offer users an experience similar to working with a therapist. In the case of Woebot, the app is programmed to help people work through challenges including anxiety and depression. The app uses artificial intelligence techniques such as recalling a person's prior responses and then tailoring new responses accordingly.

New digital mental health tools show promise in helping people better identify how their thought patterns are impacting their feelings. While behavioral health experts believe it's unlikely computers can fully replace humans in helping with mental health issues, many agree that apps can supplement other therapies such as medication and lifestyle changes to provide basic support when real humans are unavailable. Some apps, such as Better Stop Suicide and iBreathe, are free and offer assistance with very specific conditions.

Indigenous youth suffering from a mental health crisis can text NATIVE to 741741 to be connected to a trained counselor on the Native Crisis Text Line.

Warmlines

Another resource to assist people in crisis are warmlines. These are similar to hotlines, but for less urgent situations. Like crisis hotlines, warmlines allow people facing mental health challenges to find caring, trained individuals to talk with at any time of the day or night. Warmlines are typically staffed by people who have received some mental health training and who may have experienced their own mental health issues in the past.

Like crisis lines, warmlines are free to contact and the caller's identity is kept confidential. Warmlines are good options for people who want to talk about issues that are not immediate threats to their well-being. Many warmlines will refer people in crisis situations to different resources if they believe there is a better fit for the situation. Mental Health America maintains a listing of warmlines by state. Occasionally a crisis center also will offer a warmline.

Chipping Away at Stigma

Despite some progress, mental health remains the subject of stigma in many communities. This is fueled by misinformation, ignorance, and sometimes prejudice. A teen writer who identifies as S says:

> Almost all of my peers have some form of mental health disorder, they just aren't being treated for it. Saying this to someone from older generations may cause snarky comments like 'your generation is just too sensitive,' but that only strengthens my idea that older generations struggled just as much with mental health but weren't given any help.[20]

A 2021 study looked at attitudes Americans had toward mental health issues. It found that while more people are accepting of science-based causes for mental illness, that shift is not generally translating into a change in behavior. More people might understand the causes of mental health issues but still seek to avoid interacting with people who have mental illnesses. "Stigma is broad and pervasive and, up till now, has been notoriously stubborn to change efforts," said Bernice Pescosolido, a professor at Indiana University and a coauthor of the study. "Stigma translates into so many issues, including people's reluctance to seek care, our shortage of mental health professionals, and the US' unwillingness to invest resources into the mental health sector."[21]

One exception within the study results was regarding depression. Research indicated a greater acceptance of and willingness to interact with people who had depression. Conversely, the study found public attitudes toward schizophrenia and alcohol dependence went in the opposite direction, with more people viewing these illnesses as either dangerous or caused by a lack of morality. Brea Perry, another study coauthor, says:

> It is encouraging to find more progressive attitudes toward mental illness among millennials and to see public stigma around depression significantly decreasing, especially as rates of depression continue to rise in the U.S. among young people. . . . Taken as a whole, our findings support rethinking stigma and retooling stigma reduction strategies to improve public attitudes surrounding mental illness. There is a lot of work left to be done.[22]

Addressing the stigma around mental health is an important goal for many reasons. Stigma continues to discourage some people from seeking mental health care, which can lead to worsening symptoms. Stigma also can lead to feelings of

> "Stigma is broad and pervasive and, up till now, has been notoriously stubborn to change efforts. Stigma translates into so many issues, including people's reluctance to seek care, our shortage of mental health professionals, and the US' unwillingness to invest resources into the mental health sector."
>
> —Bernice Pescosolido, a professor at Indiana University

reduced hope and self-esteem among people facing mental health challenges. These feelings can make it harder for people with mental health challenges to succeed at work or in social situations.

To help fight this stigma, people can educate themselves and advocate for mental health awareness and treatment. One place to get started is with NAMI. This national nonprofit group offers free mental health support and education services. People can locate NAMI groups near them by calling or texting the NAMI helpline at 1-800-950-6264. They can also get more information on the NAMI website.

In addition, SAMHSA offers a free tool kit to start conversations about mental health. The tool kit includes a series of questions to ask in group settings, such as, "What does mental health mean to me?" or "What does mental health mean to us as a community?" With this tool kit, SAMHSA encourages school, community, and government leaders to openly discuss mental health issues, which can begin to make these issues feel more normal and acceptable.

People who haven't gone through a mental health crisis may not understand what it's like. Talking openly about mental health with caring friends can help educate them.

CHAPTER FIVE

Self-Care

Life can be stressful at any age and in any circumstance. Mental health professionals often suggest that people take steps to help them successfully manage life's twists, turns, and challenges. This practice is commonly called self-care. Self-care involves people setting aside time each day to do things that energize them and make them feel good.

Self-care looks different depending on the person, but the result is the same. "It is important to take care of ourselves so that we can show up more powerfully in our own lives and for the people we love," said Kristin Lothman, a mind-body counselor at the Mayo Clinic. "No matter how you do it, by taking time to attend to ourselves, we are intentionally creating love, safety and belonging within ourselves, which is necessary for continued resilience in and through difficult times."[23]

For people seeking to reach out to others in crisis, self-care can improve their ability to be there for others. A regular self-care practice also makes it less likely that life's challenges will result in a mental health crisis of one's own. People can make self-care part of their daily routine.

> "It is important to take care of ourselves so that we can show up more powerfully in our own lives and for the people we love."
>
> —Kristin Lothman, mind-body counselor at the Mayo Clinic

People react to stress in different ways. Some people lash out in anger or frustration. Other people may withdraw into themselves.

Help Yourself to Help Others

Self-care begins by paying attention to basic needs including food, sleep, and physical activity. Eating nutritious meals at regular times each day, engaging in regular physical activity, and getting eight to ten hours of sleep each night is ideal for maintaining mental health and resilience. Young people who establish these habits are more likely to maintain them as they get older. This can lead to improved mental health in adulthood and therefore decrease the likelihood of experiencing a mental health crisis.

Self-care doesn't need to be fancy to be effective. A teen writer identified as Z said, "Sometimes getting out of my room and going outside for even just five minutes or grabbing a healthy and fulfilling snack is beneficial to my mental health."[24] One key to success is to create and stick with a set schedule, or routine. People should start by thinking about what they want out of a routine. After some self-reflection, they might realize that they've been skipping meals, or that playing video games has been getting in the way of a good night's sleep. They could think about what a schedule would look like if sleep and regular meals were a higher priority.

It can be useful for a person to share her routine with friends and family members. She can ask them to keep her accountable for sticking with the new routine. People can also include some fun activities in their routine so it becomes more appealing to stick to it. For example, people can include physical activities that they enjoy, or schedule a regular meal with someone they like spending time with.

Also, it's best if people try to avoid structuring every minute of their day. Time management experts recommend building in fifteen to thirty minutes of open time between scheduled activities. This creates much-needed mental health breaks while providing some time to deal with surprises that may come up throughout the day.

Get Out and Get Social

It may be tempting to spend hours playing video games, viewing social media, or binge-watching the latest show. But people have an innate need to be social. Dr. Craig Sawchuk is a psychologist at the Mayo Clinic. He notes, "We are social animals by nature, so we tend to function better when we're in a community and being around others."[25]

Group activities don't have to cost money. Friends can get together and go for a nature walk, which is an opportunity to both socialize and enjoy the great outdoors.

Socializing improves mental health by preventing loneliness. School or community activities are excellent ways to get out and socialize with others. Spending time outside in nature, such as at a park, has been shown to deliver positive mental health benefits too, including reduced stress and improved mood. The healthier a person's mental health, the less likely he or she is to experience a mental health crisis.

Another way to socialize and meet new people is by volunteering. Giving to others can be an effective tool for helping people feel better about themselves and their lives. Volunteering as a young person can also lead to new skills, new connections to other people, and new inspiration about future jobs or fields of study.

In addition to group activities, people can find at least one person they trust in order to talk about things that really matter to them. For young people who have close connections with their parents or caregivers, they may be able to discuss the issues with them and solve problems together. If that is not an option, this trusted person might be a friend, a neighbor, a relative, or a mental health professional.

Mind, Body, and Mental Health

In addition to having healthy routines and social connections, regular mindfulness practices can be important tools for people in managing stress and maintaining mental health. Being mindful means a person has slowed down and really noticed his actions and feelings. Mindfulness also means taking in that information and accepting it rather than judging or dwelling on it. Mindfulness can help people react better to stressful situations and reduce depression and anxiety.

Sometimes thoughts, especially those related to fear and anxiety, are overwhelming. Being mindful can help people turn off the chatter and self-talk in their heads so they see things more clearly. Mindfulness can also help people have increased awareness of their feelings and emotions, which is a necessary first step in managing those things.

Research has shown that certain activities are effective at quieting the often noisy and sometimes distressing thoughts that can be a part of daily life. One of these activities is exercise. Just twenty minutes of intense exercise can help alleviate anxious thoughts and improve one's mood.

In addition, slowing down and experiencing the world through the senses can help clear people's heads and make them more present. Dr. Henry Emmons is an integrative psychologist who encourages this type of mindfulness activity. "I like the term *grounding* for this. Sensory experiences help us to get grounded in our bodies, a great antidote to stressful overthinking and painful feelings. When our awareness is occupied by something pleasing to our senses, such as a beautiful song or a refreshing scent, racing thoughts slow down," he said.[26]

Focused breathing and muscle relaxation exercises can also be used to address negative emotions and stress. Some research suggests that different breathing patterns can affect the brain. For instance, when people intentionally slow and deepen their breathing, such as by breathing in slowly, holding it, then breathing out even more slowly, this signals the body and the brain to calm down. Practicing this technique in a noncrisis situation will help people become familiar and comfortable with it. That way, if they are ever in a crisis, they can use this technique to help regulate their emotions.

Focused muscle relaxation exercises can also help people manage stress. These exercises help people become aware of where they might be holding stress or tension within their bodies.

RAIN

It's normal for people to want to avoid facing difficult and uncomfortable feelings, such as worry or fear. However, not addressing those feelings does not make them go away. Decades ago, meditation instructor Michele McDonald developed a mindfulness tool to help people be more aware and understanding of their uncomfortable emotions and reframe them to be less disruptive. She called it Recognize, Allow, Investigate, and Non-identification (RAIN).

RAIN is a mindfulness practice that can be useful when a person is feeling stressed or overwhelmed. *Recognizing* means consciously acknowledging and naming current emotions without judging them as good or bad. *Allowing* is giving permission for the feelings to exist instead of immediately seeking to change them. *Investigating* involves looking at the emotions through the lens of curiosity, almost like a scientist. Adding this distance allows people to identify how the emotions are presenting in the physical body instead of the mind. Finally, *non-identification* reinforces that people are not their thoughts, and thoughts routinely come and go as life progresses.

In addition to releasing tension, these exercises force the mind to focus on something other than negative emotions, such as fear or worry.

Activities such as yoga and tai chi present opportunities for moving meditations by focusing attention on body movements as opposed to troubling thoughts. There are many opportunities to try out these practices, as well as meditative breathing and guided muscle relaxation exercises, through free, follow-along internet videos. "The brain likes patterns, so if you are continually visualizing yourself in a calm, happy place, your brain will begin to do this on its own in time," said Kimberly Quinn, a psychology professor at Champlain College.[27]

A critical part of self-care involves a person figuring out what she loves to do and making sure she dedicates at least a little time to it every day. To start, she can make a list of small things that make her happy. It could be as simple as taking a dog for a walk, listening to music, or enjoying a warm drink. Then she can adjust her daily routine to make sure she includes those things. A consistent self-care routine can help people avoid mental health challenges down the road. It also helps make people better prepared to assist others who may be experiencing challenges.

The Brain on Meditation

Meditation helps decrease anxiety and stress. Modern medicine offers a host of diagnostic tools that have allowed psychologists and neurologists to better understand what happens in the brain during meditation. One finding indicates that meditation can help a person intentionally turn down his or her sympathetic nervous system, which is responsible for the fight-or-flight response. At the same time, meditation allows a person to intentionally turn up the parasympathetic nervous system, which is associated with a calm, resting state. Like any skill, however, it takes practice before a person can enjoy the full effects. With time and regular practice, even ten or fifteen minutes of mindfulness meditation can help a person feel better.

Listening to a favorite upbeat song may improve a person's mood. Pairing this with an activity, such as a walk, can make a person feel even better.

Using Music for Self-Care

Music is a powerful self-care tool. Research has found that when people listen to music they enjoy, their brain releases dopamine, a feel-good hormone. Lorrie Kubicek is a music therapist. She notes:

> The use of music interventions (listening to music, singing, and music therapy) can create significant improvements in mental health, and smaller improvements in physical health. . . . Listening [to music] can be done with intentional focus or as background listening. You can amplify emotions for release. You can use music to quiet the mind. Or you can . . . match music to your current energy or mood, and then slowly change feel, tempo, and complexity to help you shift. Music listening can be paired with prompts for relaxation, or to motivate you to exercise, move more, or do a task you've been putting off.[28]

Self-care routines can benefit from music in several ways. Listening to at least one favorite song each day can be an immediate mood booster. This effect is especially noticeable if the song has positive associations for the listener. To reduce stress, people can try listening to slower-paced songs.

People who make music can receive a double boost to their emotional well-being. Making music—along with other creative activities including visual and performing arts, crafts, and even mindful coloring—have been shown to help reduce stress and anxiety. Expressing oneself creatively also can provide a jolt of positive energy and excitement.

> "The use of music interventions (listening to music, singing, and music therapy) can create significant improvements in mental health, and smaller improvements in physical health."
> — Lorrie Kubicek, music therapist

Put It on Paper

Writing is one way that people can process overwhelming emotions, such as worry or fear. Getting feelings out of one's head and onto paper can be therapeutic and eye-opening. Daily journaling is a proven self-care tool to help relieve anxiety and stress, especially for people who are recovering from traumatic events. Journaling is also a vehicle for unloading thoughts and feelings into a safe, nonjudgmental place.

Experts suggest that people schedule ten to twenty minutes in their daily routines for this activity. They should write in a place where they're comfortable. A nice notebook or journal may encourage people to do this activity and maintain the routine. People should write without stopping. They should let their emotions and thoughts pour out unobstructed. Journals are places for honesty, not judgment.

People can also list things they're thankful for. Those things could be people, places, activities, or even feelings. Research has shown that a regular gratitude practice helps people feel more positive.

Maintaining good mental health requires awareness, skill-building, and education. Self-care and mindfulness can help people weather life's challenges. People who are aware of their own mental health and have developed practices to keep it functioning at peak performance are in a good position to be there for others who might be experiencing a mental health crisis.

Journaling allows people to explore and examine their feelings.

SOURCE NOTES

Introduction: A Spotlight on Mental Health

1. Quoted in Erica Gonzalez, "Meghan Markle Said She 'Didn't Want to Be Alive Anymore' During Her Lowest Moments as a Royal," *Harper's Bazaar*, March 7, 2021. www.harpersbazaar.com.

2. Quoted in "Meghan Markle Said She 'Didn't Want to Be Alive Anymore' During Her Lowest Moments as a Royal."

3. Quoted in LMT, "How Prince Harry Helped Meghan at Her Worst Point," *YouTube*, October 11, 2022. www.youtube.com.

4. Quoted in Elise Taylor, "Prince Harry and Meghan Markle Intimately Detail Why They Left the Royal Family," *Vogue*, December 15, 2022. www.vogue.com.

Chapter One: Hidden Struggles

5. Quoted in "Protecting Youth Mental Health," *US Department of Health and Human Services*, 2021. www.hhs.gov.

6. Quoted in TEDx Talks, "The Truth About Teen Depression," *YouTube*, February 6, 2015. www.youtube.com.

7. Quoted in Matt Richtel, "'It's Life or Death': The Mental Health Crisis Among U.S. Teens," *New York Times*, May 3, 2022. www.nytimes.com.

8. Quoted in Matt Richtel, "Surgeon General Warns of Youth Mental Health Crisis," *New York Times*, December 7, 2021. www.nytimes.com.

9. Holly R. Farley, "Assessing Mental Health in Vulnerable Adolescents," *Nursing*, October 2020. https://journals.lww.com.

Chapter Two: Preparing to Reach Out

10. Quoted in Miranda Spencer, "Understanding the Youth Mental Health Crisis: An Interview with Elia Abi-Jaoude." *Mad in America*, January 19, 2022. www.madinamerica.com.

11. Quoted in "Why Mental Health Care Is Stigmatized in Black Communities," *USC Suzanne Dworak-Peck*, February 12, 2019. https://dworakpeck.usc.edu.

12. Luna Greenstein, "How to Help Someone in Crisis," *NAMI* (blog), September 20, 2017. www.nami.org.

Chapter Three: Starting a Conversation

13. Quoted in Rhitu Chatterjee, "Reach Out and Listen: How to Help Someone at Risk of Suicide," *NPR*, December 22, 2022. www.npr.org.

14. Quoted in Matt Richtel, "How to Help Teens Struggling with Mental Health," *New York Times*, April 27, 2022. www.nytimes.com.

15. Quoted in Arlin Cuncic, "What Is Active Listening?" *VeryWellMind*, November 9, 2022. www.verywellmind.com.

16. Quoted in "Reach Out and Listen: How to Help Someone at Risk of Suicide."

17. "How to Help Someone in Crisis," *NAMI* (blog), September 20, 2017. www.nami.org.

Chapter Four: Caring Connections

18. Quoted in Dani Blum, "What to Know About 988, the New Mental Health Crisis Hotline," *New York Times*, July 12, 2022. www.nytimes.com.

19. Quoted in Megan Leonhardt, "What You Need to Know About the Cost and Accessibility of Mental Health Care in America," *CNBC*, May 10, 2021. www.cnbc.com.

20. Quoted in "What Students Are Saying About Teen Mental Health, Moderating Speech and Special Talents," *New York Times*, May 12, 2022. www.nytimes.com.

21. Quoted in "Stigma Surrounding Depression Drops for First Time in U.S. but Increases for Other Mental Illnesses," *News at IU*, December 21, 2021. https://news.iu.edu.

22. Quoted in "Stigma Surrounding Depression Drops for First Time in U.S. but Increases for Other Mental Illnesses."

Chapter Five: Self-Care

23. Quoted in Cynthia Weiss, "Self-Care Tips to Manage Mental Health and Wellness," *Mayo Clinic News Network*, January 31, 2021. https://newsnetwork.mayoclinic.org.

24. Quoted in "What Students Are Saying About Teen Mental Health, Moderating Speech and Special Talents."

25. Quoted in Vivien William, "Mayo Clinic Minute: The Benefits of Being Socially Connected," *Mayo Clinic News Network*, April 19, 2019. https://newsnetwork.mayoclinic.org.

26. Quoted in "How Using Your Senses Can Improve Your Mental Health," *Frank Lipman MD*, September 9, 2022. https://drfranklipman.com.

27. Quoted in Denise Mann, "What Is Guided Meditation? Here Are the Benefits and How to Get Started," *Healthy*, January 7, 2022. www.thehealthy.com.

28. Lorrie Kubicek, "Can Music Improve Our Health and Quality of Life?" *Harvard Health Publishing* (blog), July 25, 2022. www.health.harvard.edu.

FOR FURTHER RESEARCH

Books

Kristina C. Castillo, *Anxiety and Depression on the Rise*. San Diego, CA: ReferencePoint Press, 2023.

Kristi Hugstad, *Beneath the Surface: A Teen's Guide to Reaching Out When You or Your Friend Is in Crisis*. Novato, CA: New World Library, 2019.

Carla Mooney, *Getting Help: Coping With and Overcoming Mental Illness*. San Diego, CA: ReferencePoint Press, 2023.

Internet Sources

"Incorporate Mindfulness into Your Life," *Mindfulness for Teens*, n.d. www.mindfulnessforteens.com.

"Mental Health," *CDC*, September 12, 2022. www.cdc.gov.

"SAMHSA's National Helpline," *SAMHSA*, n.d. www.samhsa.gov.

"Teen Mental Health," *MedlinePlus*, n.d. https://medlineplus.gov.

Related Organizations

American Academy of Child and Adolescent Psychiatry

www.aacap.org

The American Academy of Child and Adolescent Psychiatry has a Youth Resources web page. It gives teens information about mental illnesses, how they can get help, and how to advocate for themselves and others.

National Alliance on Mental Illness (NAMI)

www.nami.org

NAMI advocates for people with mental illnesses with the goal of ensuring they can live healthy lives. This organization also educates the public on mental illnesses.

National Institute of Mental Health (NIMH)

www.nimh.nih.gov

The NIMH provides in-depth information regarding mental illnesses and the latest research in the mental health field.

INDEX

IMAGE CREDITS

ABOUT THE AUTHOR

Jill C. Wheeler is the author of more than 300 nonfiction titles for young readers. Her interests include behavioral sciences, sustainable agriculture, and any kind of travel. She lives in Minneapolis, Minnesota, where she enjoys sailing, riding motorcycles, and reading.